I0786575

All the Best
Medallions

50 drawings by Joan Worth
From the Wallflowers Series – Volume #4

©2018 Joan Worth De Pere, Wisconsin
ISBN-13: 978-1725593763
ISBN-10: 1725593769

All the Best Medallions * from the Wallflowers Series #4 ©2018 Joan Worth

All the Best Medallions * from the Wallflowers Series #4 ©2018 Joan Worth

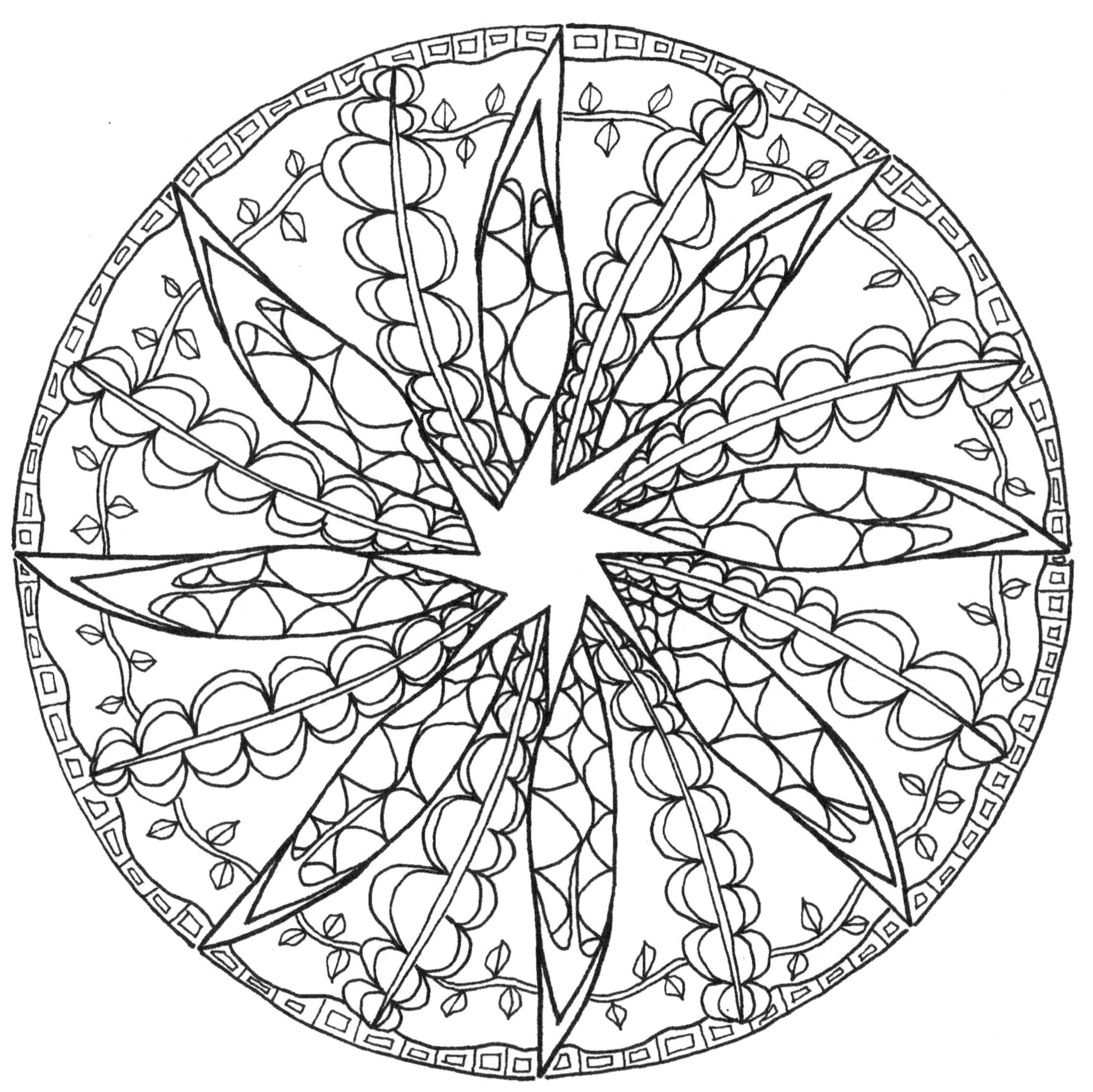

All the Best Medallions * from the Wallflowers Series #4 ©2018 Joan Worth

All the Best Medallions * from the Wallflowers Series #4 ©2018 Joan Worth

All the Best Medallions * from the Wallflowers Series #4 ©2018 Joan Worth

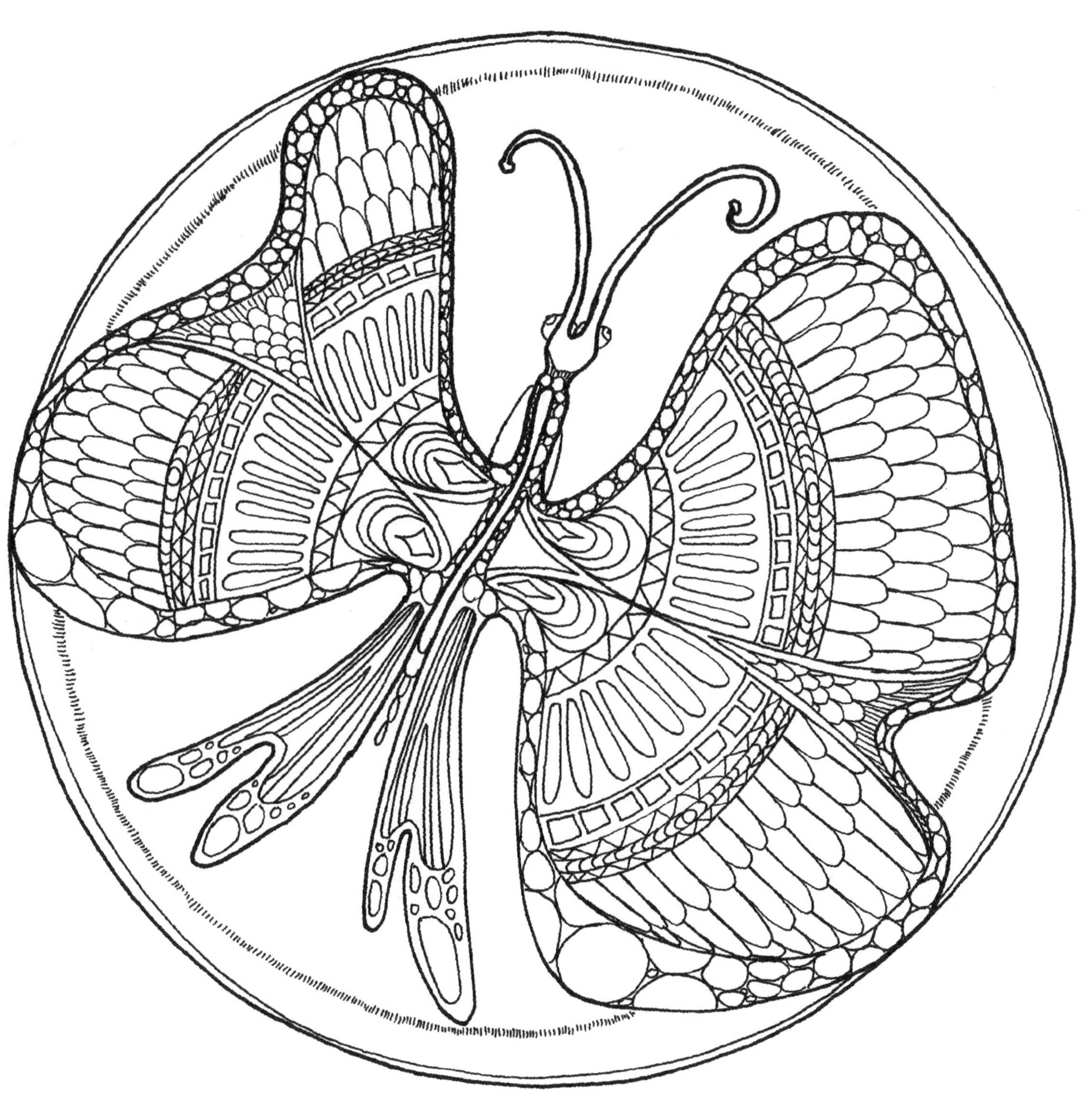

All the Best Medallions * from the Wallflowers Series #4 ©2018 Joan Worth

All the Best Medallions * from the Wallflowers Series #4 ©2018 Joan Worth

All the Best Medallions * from the Wallflowers Series #4 ©2018 Joan Worth

All the Best Medallions * from the Wallflowers Series #4 ©2018 Joan Worth

All the Best Medallions * from the Wallflowers Series #4 ©2018 Joan Worth

All the Best Medallions * from the Wallflowers Series #4 ©2018 Joan Worth

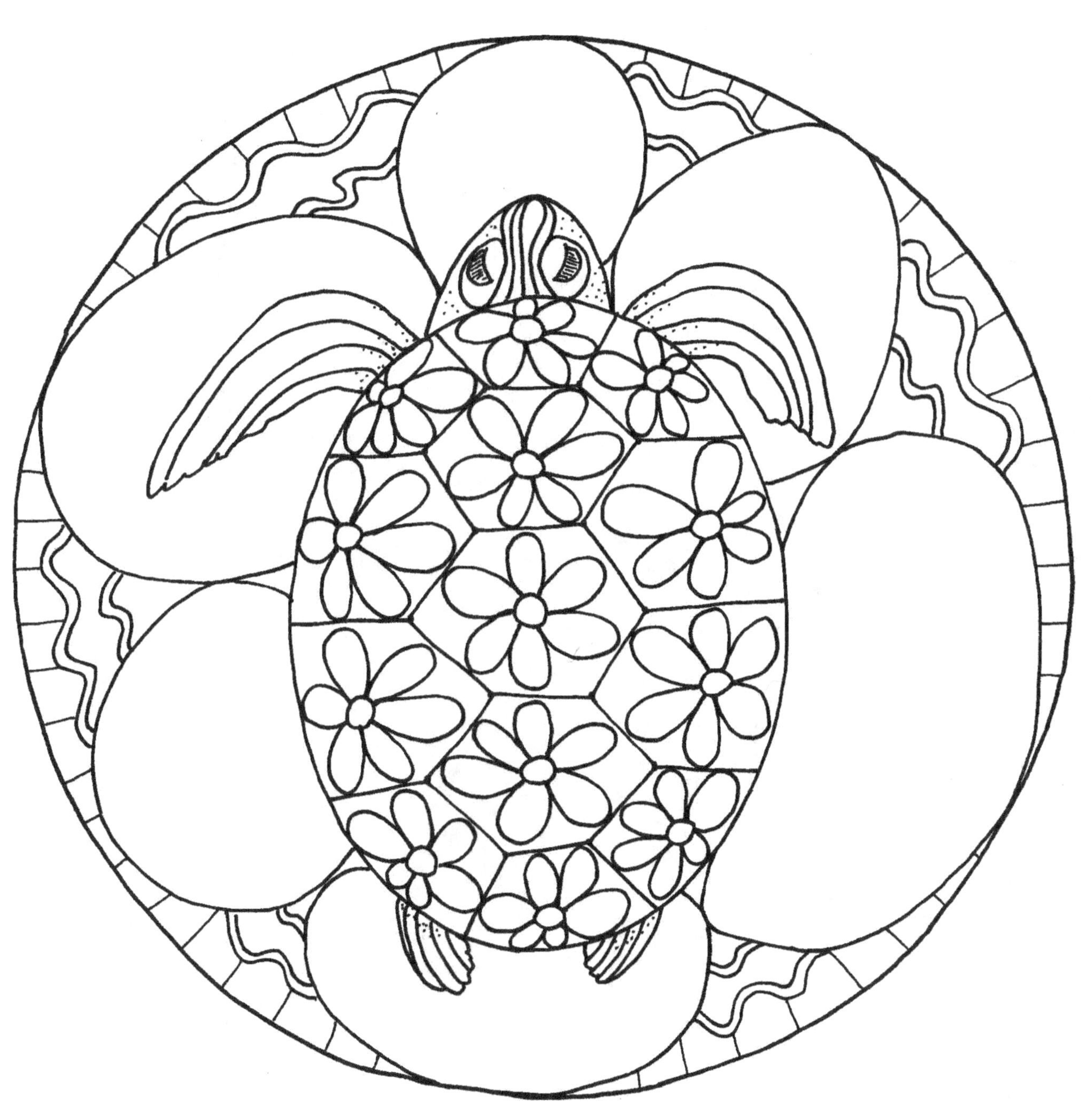

All the Best Medallions * from the Wallflowers Series #4 ©2018 Joan Worth

All the Best Medallions * from the Wallflowers Series #4 ©2018 Joan Worth

All the Best Medallions * from the Wallflowers Series #4 ©2018 Joan Worth

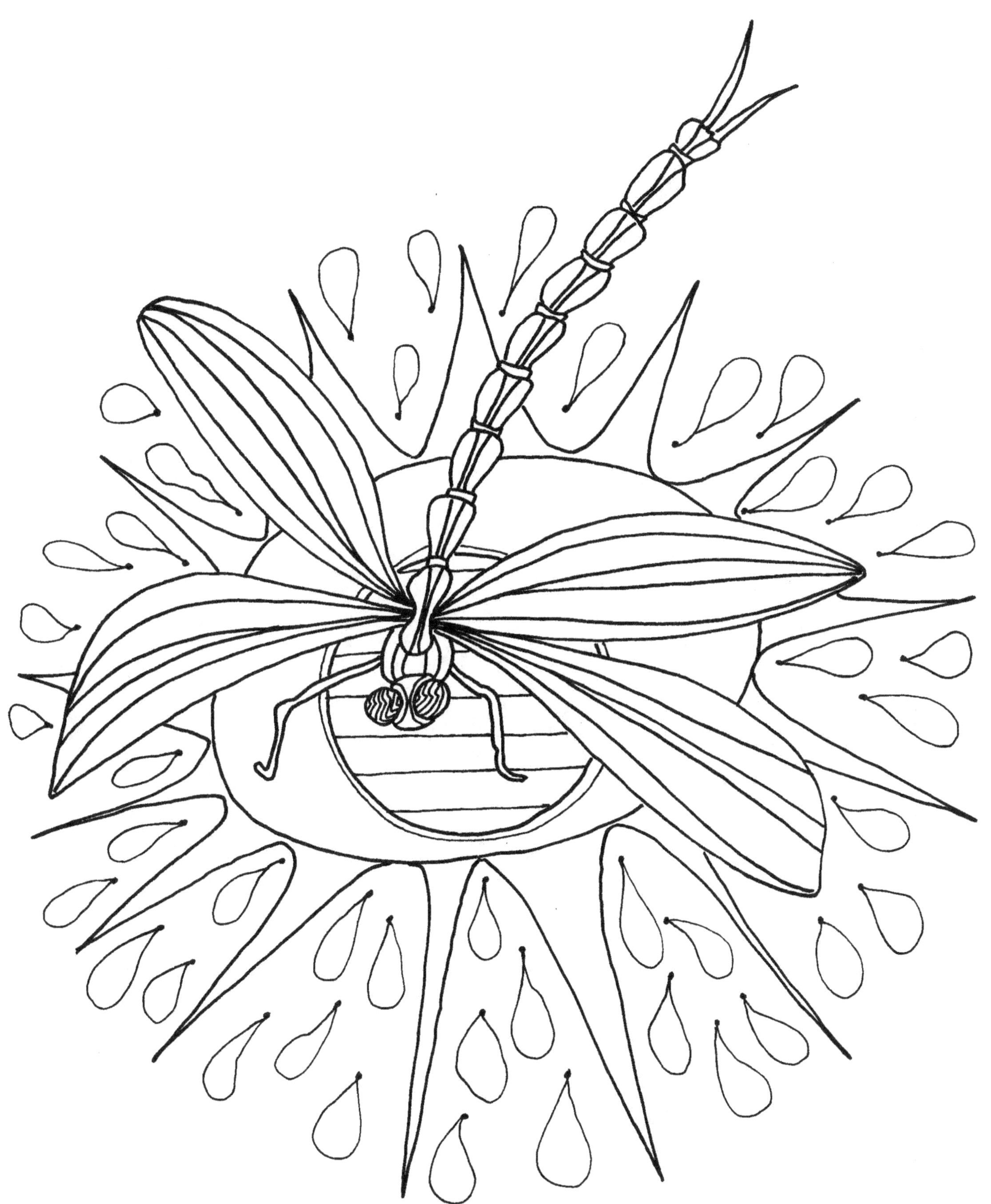

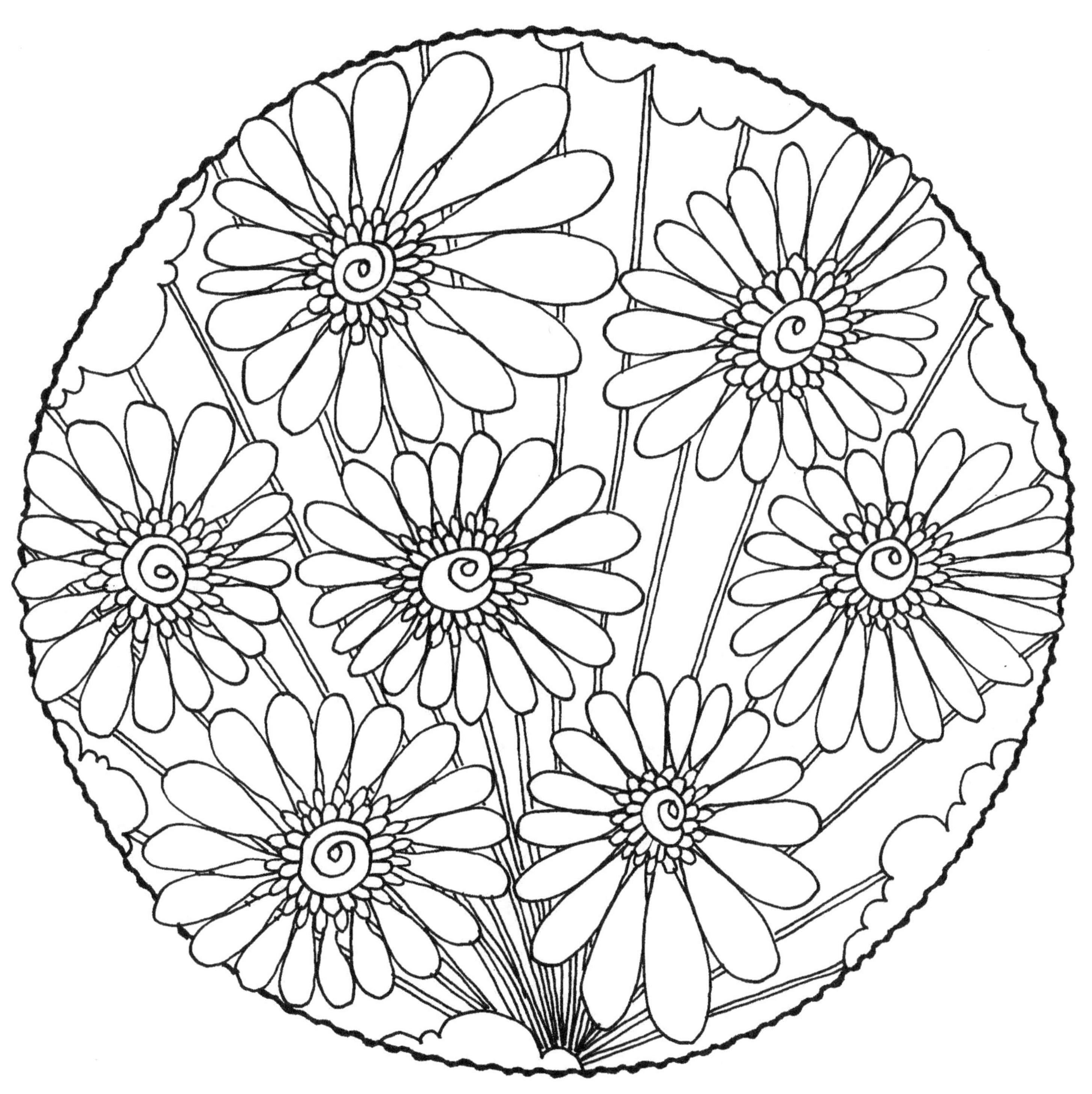

All the Best Medallions * from the Wallflowers Series #4 ©2018 Joan Worth

All the Best Medallions * from the Wallflowers Series #4 ©2018 Joan Worth

All the Best Medallions * from the Wallflowers Series #4 ©2018 Joan Worth

All the Best Medallions * from the Wallflowers Series #4 ©2018 Joan Worth

All the Best Medallions * from the Wallflowers Series #4 ©2018 Joan Worth

All the Best Medallions * from the Wallflowers Series #4 ©2018 Joan Worth

All the Best Medallions * from the Wallflowers Series #4 ©2018 Joan Worth

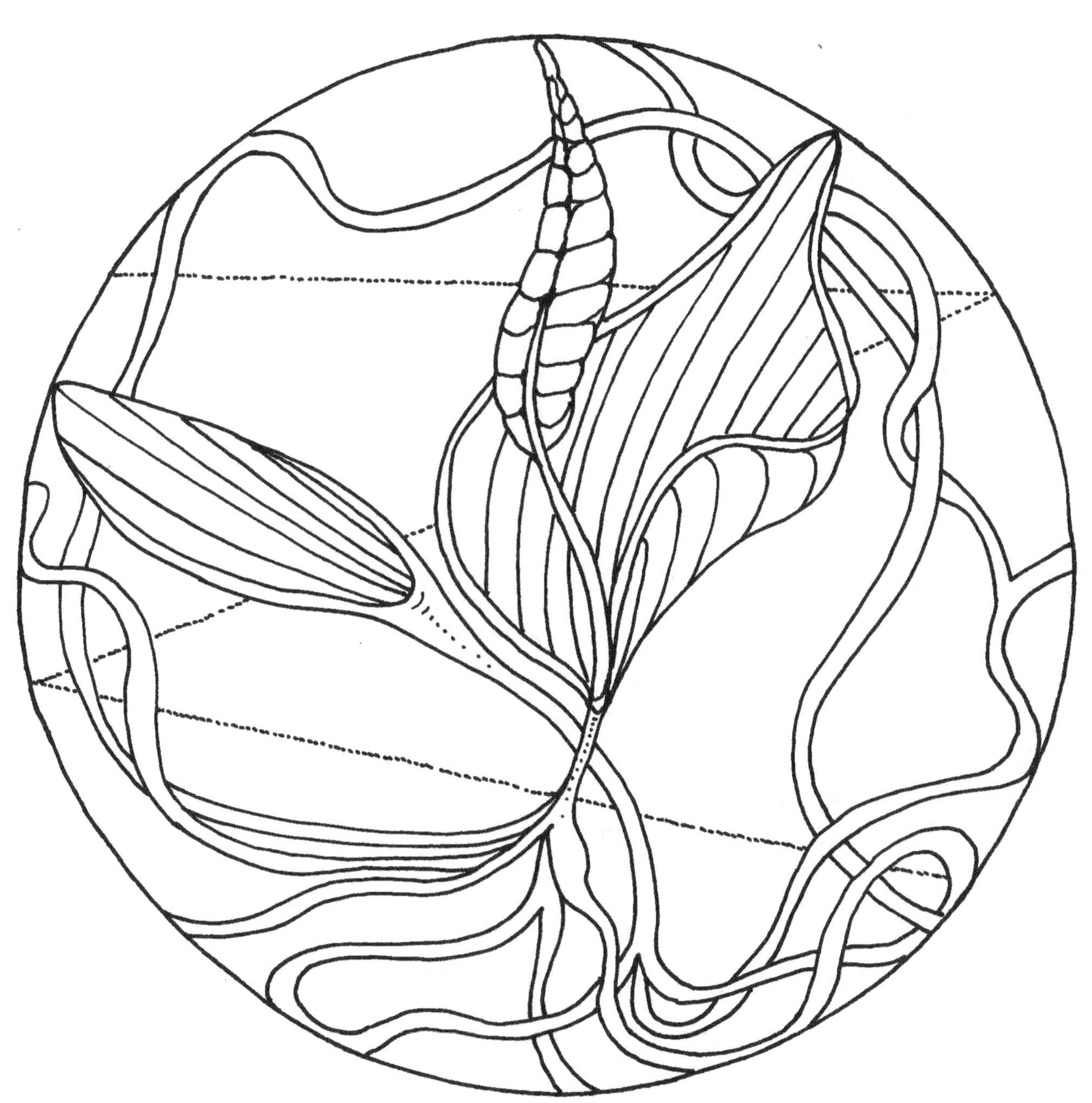

All the Best Medallions * from the Wallflowers Series #4 ©2018 Joan Worth

All the Best Medallions * from the Wallflowers Series #4 ©2018 Joan Worth

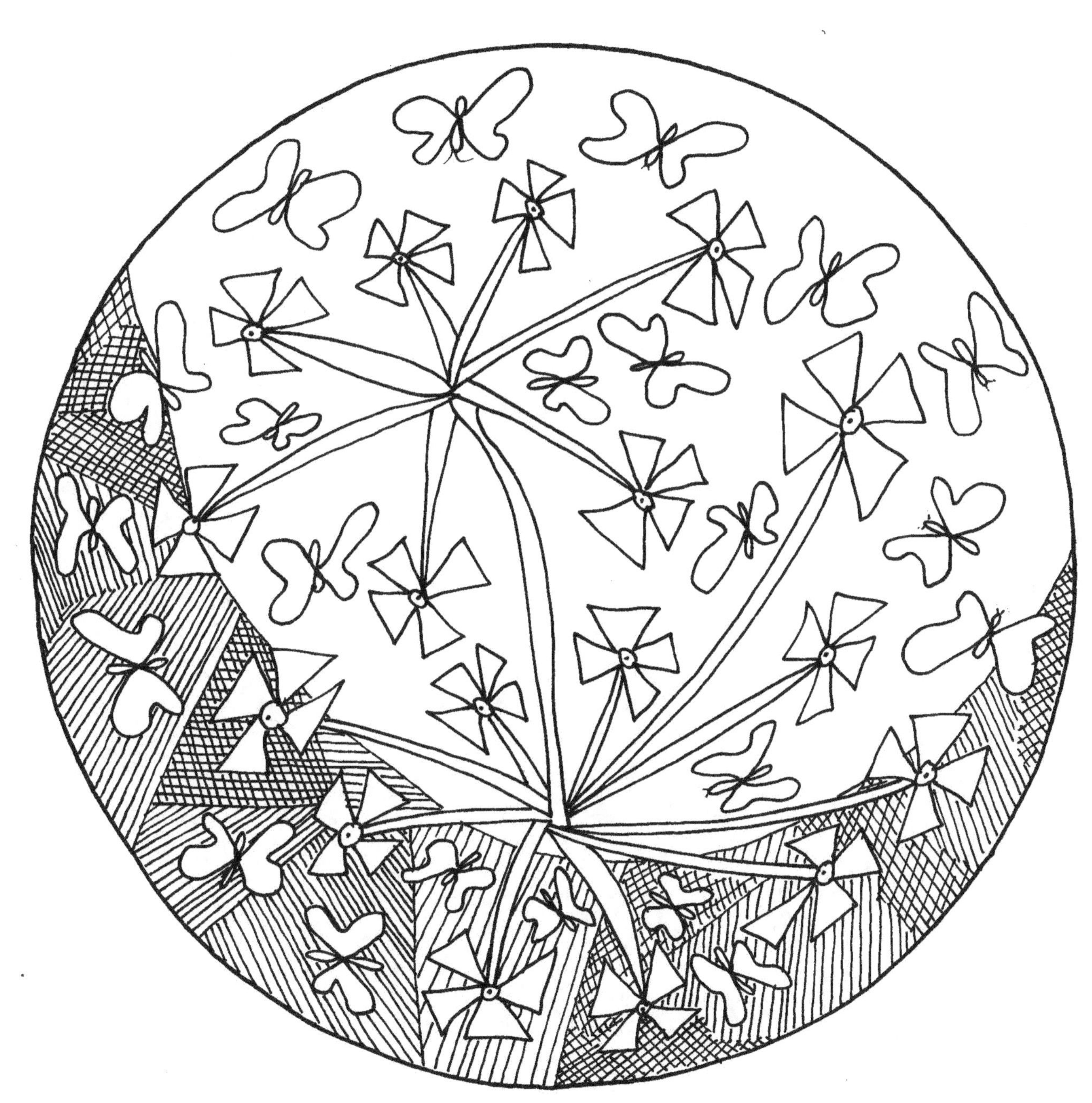

All the Best Medallions * from the Wallflowers Series #4 ©2018 Joan Worth

All the Best Medallions * from the Wallflowers Series #4 ©2018 Joan Worth

All images taken from the
Wallflowers Series

Wallflowers Volume #1
Pages 1-15
Wallflowers #2 volume #2
Pages 16-30
Pick Me Volume #3
Pages 31-50